kiss & release

poems by

Anthony DiPietro

For information contact:
Unsolicited Press
Portland, Oregon
www.unsolicitedpress.com
orders@unsolicitedpress.com
619-354-8005

Cover Design: Kathryn Gerhardt
Editor: S.R. Stewart

ISBN: 978-1-956692-87-7

contents

nations are warring 92% of the time

kiss & release

yes & when

when I was an uber driver,

friends asked for my horror stories. I said my scariest customers were four young republican lawyers, drunk from a long day of golf. pickup at pine brook country club, heading home to newton highlands. the one guy looking at the back of my head had ordered the car. each of his three buds stumbled across their green lawns to kiss their wives with reeking breath. after they left, my customer said, my friends are not bad guys, which told me he thought they were real assholes. he was sorry they talked about golf vs. tennis & which was a real man's sport. I said golf is not the most important thing in life, but there are worse things you could say in someone's back seat. very level-headed of you, he said, I like you, I'd back you for congress. then he asked what I thought of the gun debate. I knew not to answer. uber driver training was only a nine-minute youtube vid, but it distinctly said, never venture into politics or religion. instead, I steered the conversation to where we grew up & that's how we realized that will & I went to the same college, him two years behind me. he was the one who hosted a foursome once at his dorm, all guys, & I left in the middle. I wanted the hot one for myself. the other two were boring. I had encountered will one other time, in the basement restroom of the research library. there was I, hard in his soft cheeks, holding his pierced ears, giving him the rhythm, his small, toothy mouth not doing a great job. but he was really trying.

wallflower's complaint

I wish I knew a way to cheat with dance.
my hips won't find the rhythm. this always told me
the mirror ball scene is not my lover.
sure I shake in back when I'm certain no one
can see, like I sing when I'm driving around
until my mother calls & mentions ice. be careful,

her favorite phrase in funny accent. be cahful
going up/down stairs, getting in & out of bed. you'll dance
straight to the e.r. mister. (she don't mess around.)
dad worries I suck dick. our priest always told me
clean jokes. priests can't play favorites. this blue-eyed one
surely did, & saintly he was not. my son,

he'd say, with warm, neutral breath (he's not my lover;
this breath imagined). when I outgrew be careful
I landed a bearded, bluer-eyed someone
to grip, lick, spit & slip, locked in the dance
I'd heard so much about. girls always told me
in high school, you will marry young. I sleep around

now. they guessed right. at 22, sex rolled around
on sat a.m. like milk delivered. wasn't my lover
a specimen, if humdrum? he always told me

platitudes. warnings? if you come home early, be careful
how quickly you enter. you may find two men dance
deep in the plush queen bed you share with one.

which isn't, strictly speaking, why it went to shit, but one
reason I neither listened nor trusted. floor's not ground,
I found out, the boards shift. the dance
I've learned best is avoidance. he who's not my lover
never was, his name redacted. I must be careful
what I confess to myself. the poets always told me

hard truths. my cheeks, pits, pelvis blazed always. told me
what to pack & pointed west whenever one
more highway called. thieves emptied cash from my socks,
never careful
to wait & see drugs take effect, never stuck around
till the film's climax: father swearing, you/this is not my son.
the sequence repeated, my 20s & 30s one long dance

I'd sooner forget. I recall who always told me, don't dance
with just anyone. I heard, don't find just one lover, son.
when you love, be careful. talk right & walk. don't swish
around.

fuckboy (first night)

you arrived (swooped around the corner like a bat) five
        mins before my laundry timer rang (let it wrinkle
or tumble on like sisyphus's rock) a stew
        was on the stove (let it burn) I'll scrape black char
from the ruined pot (another night) I never need to eat again
        (now that the whole house burns around us)
satan's minions surround us (demented mentors)
        while you coach me to choke you a little (slap you
a little harder now) now the other cheek (did I
        summon them with my red light) or did you
(who's in charge now) I can't stop pleasing you
        if I wanted to (can't stop hurting you if I wanted to)
I can't stop the knowledge you are in charge of how
        powerful you make me feel (& how I make you feel)
you beg me to keep going (every time I rest)
        I go to the fridge for water (& you come
wearing my robe) the leftover chinese food containers
        wait to be thrown out (I realize they are from my life
before you were my ruler) at some point
        I ask (your name) you give yourself (the name
of a famous brit lit character) you consider
        letting me rename you (without
closing the bathroom door) you evacuate
        & wipe (in front of me) I know we've put everything

backwards (we've already fallen in love)

     which is the most important thing (so now tell me)

everything else (I should know about you)

who do you think you are?

did you ever try on your mother's high heels? did you prefer red? did you like the smell of nail polish remover? could you make eye contact on the school bus? when you looked at older boys did you notice their body hair patterns? can you still recall your mother's friend's nephew stretching on a diving board? didn't you notice cousin paul was in gram's words a little artistic? which parent went to bed first every night? which would wake to stoke the fire in winter & crack open watermelon in summer? why did you hate the day of the week that smelled like cinnamon buns? do you remember the first time you unzipped a man's jeans? whose couch were you on? when you moved to california how did you choose which city? when you came back why did you leave again? are you the kind of person who stays friends with your exes? after three years with your partner why did you kiss someone else at a party? what did you eat while your lover was too enraged to look at you? why did you try to buy a dog & live in a suburb? were you or were you not a workaholic like your father? where was the first wedding when you felt old? who visited you in your next apartment? did you wear a condom every time? were you already used to the quiet? how did you keep your spider plant alive? which was fuller your refrigerator or your freezer? how many times do you intend to move? did you really think that was love?

love is finished again (1st movement)

strike the center
of a silence
with a low
resonant gong
your ears
can't tell
exactly when
its sound
has ended
& another
has taken over

love is finished again like that

*

*

like a thing you can't remember
      whether you said aloud or merely thought

like a specific drive you arrive without memory of
      because you ride the same route over & over

like a window left open during rain
      witnessed later in its wetness & slid shut

*

*

you would think
that lightning
wouldn't strike
twice but
it often
does in the very
same place
love is finished
again
a repeat
lightning strike

*

a letter to my therapist while I am high

I'll kill love so dead that
       it never comes back
             I swear I'll do it
                 look out
every good love story has murder inside it
       james baldwin knew that
             does murder equal love?
                 is the true secret this thing
too dark to learn that by killing a thing
       or a person you become them?
             like eating like we lay to waste
                 molecules energy knowledge
& if this is true
       what is this hunger?
             later I'll be embarrassed to read this
                 but I'll still turn & turn this idea
obsessed like a knife shucking oysters & burn
       like the holiest god
             don't you dare come
                 any closer madness
to my mind for I know
       what you want madness
             I can smell you like one of my own
                 men I spend time inside

yet remain unknown like medicine
      or music or the weight
           of packs of bricks he takes out
               of his heart at night while I throw
& catch daggers oblivious to the hurt
      this is too many explosive epiphanies
          to survive in daylight
              & clrly I'll never express what I feel
in a brief sigh of yes & when
      some man from the neighborhood is next
          upon my doorstep I will ask
             do you pray?
I'll say stand back I am dangerous
      as any change you've faced
          for I don't know where my next
            meal will come from

the whatever store on route 111

their customer's a white man

skinny & from his weight I'd say
makes nineteen five a year has sixty four k

in student debt & maybe never finished
the degree he sees his three year old son alternate saturdays

the museum costs 20 with expired student i.d. & they need
a free place to be the whatever

has so many shelves of what nobody in this
country values they don't stock guns

or mortgages

no fireworks

corporate ladders or

american flags

since this patron clerks at the district attorney's
office he checks the fast growing ethics section

they've added the t to the lgb rights pile
of black lives while the dignity section

shrinks but has the most variety

self-worth

feminism

body positivity

human life

next aisle over you can buy healthcare plans
which does come in handy his medical doesn't

have vision & his glasses were stolen
from his car on christmas near the middle

of the sales floor you find hometown history
& this country's as told in books & a child's education

is always in stock the largest single item for sale

in the vast warehouse is the arctic
ice shelf quite a spectacle to see it

glisten & melt there & I haven't
mentioned it but have you thought about

how the toddler feels touching these things
turning them over in his hands? his dad figures

in his head when the next paycheck comes & says ok
buddy we can't afford these but when we get to the checkout

I'll let you pick any one thing.

21st century love song

a cento

Yellow diamonds in the light, honey
      & milk under your tongue.
            The smell of your garments like the smell of
Lebanon, every inch of your skin
       a holy grail. Look, you have doves' eyes, & our bed
          is green. You make me feel,
you make me know, call your name 2, 3 times in a row,
       wake you up in the middle of the night
          to say: Arise my fair one, come away.
I wanna wake up in a different city. I will go up to
     the palm tree. I will take hold of its boughs. When I
        wrap my arms around you, every mistake
we make crumbles. My arms won't be any use at all
     if I can't hold you. Comfort me with apples.
         The moon was paper white
the night you saved my life.
     Now winter is past, the rain over & gone.
        Another sun-soaked season, the time of
          singing of birds
is come. Speak on it, babe, tell me
     what do you need? I tried to be chill,
        my soul failed. You have ravished my heart.
I look cute at the end

of your leash, your adorable beast. Your hair
            is like a flock of goats from Mount Gilead.
Your teeth like a flock of sheep
        which came up from the washing.
                Imma get your heart racing in my skin-tight
            jeans.
Let us go forth into the field, let's see
        whether tender grapes appear & pomegranates
                bud forth: there will I give you my loves
& I'll give you the rest of me, too.
        God is good. He took His time when
                He designed ya baby. Your lips like a thread
of scarlet. & his banner over me was love.
        You talk to me & it comes
                off the walls, your belly like a heap of wheat
set about with lilies by the rivers of waters, washed
        with milk. I used to be commander in chief of my
                pimp ship, flyin' high. My head is filled
with dew. O daughters of Jerusalem, don't wake my love!
        For love is strong
            as death: Tell the bed
not to lay like the open mouth of a grave.
        Many waters cannot quench
            love; neither can floods
drown it. When I was two & a half, my momma said to me:
        Love is funny, you will laugh,
            till the day you turn three.

came & made

while listening to 'the young person's guide to the orchestra'

benjamin britten's 'variations & fugue on a theme of purcell'

A—*whole orchestra*

> once upon a time a country
> every country had its king
> & every king a war a war is
> armies marching toward each other
> where there is war there is something
> the king aims to steal
> do you remember shalt not steal?
> an army's made of soldiers
> every soldier has her weeping mother

B—*woodwinds*

> & where there will be pain there will be love
> lovebirds sing all night then part at dawn
> if it is morning you will hear doves pray
> for peace for peace is like a country
> something we imagine & believe in
> like a magic trick & words are also tricky

fox runs & river runs
not the same way

C—*brass*

rivers can be crossed by wading
or swimming or else by tunnel or bridge depending
bridge is man-made unlike cold
& cold can be the enemy
enemy means crossed but not the same way
this you will understand one day

D—*strings*

because library you have learned is
like church except thou shalt not candles
flame is sometimes called
eternal but it must not last
which is like love & not like war
a mother's grief outlasts her handkerchief
& flags draped on her lost son's coffin

E—*percussion*

our grandmothers hoarded sympathy cards
their houses were mostly made of paper
paper & wood two traditional gifts

both hold dreams but not the same way
& dream can be someone you love
or never met or often someone lost

F—*the return*

to die I know you understand
you know it like my hand when we cross rivers
it gets windy where we cross
all answers have questions
what did you first ask? oh yes an army
is made of soldiers
if they meet they kill
do you remember shalt not kill?

the violent bear it *spoiler alert **trigger warning

at the end of the novel I want to know
why flannery o'connor raped her
main character tarwater
I ponder it on a random wednesday

lying in sunshine in an urban driveway
w/cider beer in hand & the woman
I don't know who lives below us
bellows angrily down the street

did he deserve it for drowning his dim-
witted cousin compared to a beast
throughout the text? was it revenge
or revelation? & if you live in a city

you know how this goes there are
too many of us now you have certainly heard
a woman scream or two men on a sidewalk
where you were scurrying by & you

w/back hair standing up surely walked
not toward the chaos but away
I go upstairs deciding not to think
any more today about people

doing evil & what would go really nice
w/my salad is steak tips I remember
a grown son w/just such a knife
killed his father during supper at their dinner table

on a street where kid me played all summer
& what o'connor doesn't show us
what kind of man does tarwater become?
I write in my journal we leave

this world when it becomes too dangerous
for us I read the poem that ends
now how can that be child?
how can that be?

anything you can do

what i learned as an urban gay man
is this: they are always so generous

during the ritual kiss of hello
they can pass a tab of ecstasy
from tongue to tongue unnoticed
by any third man in the room
who lightly fingers the ivory keys
& they come prepared the burliest
bear at the firemen's ball
always carries a clacker fan & his partner
offers the vape pen
or poppers from his pocket
i swear on my pearls

the skills they have
i do not mean the obvious fashion & art
tho they'll compose a symphony on iphone
on board the sinking titanic

i mean like removing a nightclub wristband
without using teeth & pouring a beer
in control of head of foam
they are book makers

dungeons & dragons game masters
they have fixed my wheel alignment
flown my plane
        & cured my chlamydia
it was a cinch

& some are even architects!
        (never mind that they're know-it-alls)
they build bridges
erections that actually move & improve
        the sight lines of ocean & sky
& palm tree views which are already always
changing anyway
        gay guys just came &
made & did it a whole lot
better

hi-nrg edm & me

this is a poem that takes place in an empty black cube for dancing,
this is a warehouse in brooklyn, or was, in polluted gowanus, this
is in fashion, are you ready for the beats? are you ready for the red
flash after blue? for the fog machine? this is a party I get to first, I
keep my clothes on, order vodka soda, try to look bored, don't
have to try, there's ethan, my instagram boyfriend, his penis I've
seen on screen, but his voice I never heard, he sings hello, he knows
jacob, wait, jacob's not traveling? c'mere for your hug, he knows
frederick, who kisses on the mouth with his eyes open wide like
the time I asked about his scar, sounds like it was bad, I said, yeah
it was, & avery's here too, sleepy-eyed like he's been smoking, then
clive & jack arrive, time to strip from jeans to beach shorts,
lifeguard red, the men like that, & standard black harness on top,
want a hit of poppers? this is called a circuit, if you don't know
how to dance, you're not alone, if you try to dance alone, there
isn't room, ethan admits he's here with a date, but you never know
how the night will end, jacob's friends are cool, nico likes my fur,
I dig his mane, I make sure he repeats my name, you're so trashy,
he says, these drinks feel weak, but I can't stop, I want to be trashy,
they've pulled back the rope to an upstairs room, but they're
shining flashlights up there, no one wants to get caught with a dick
hanging out, there are designers here, painters tracing sweat lines
on my body, brooklyn's where the artists live, this is any saturday,
a dance that's not a prom & not a wedding, not for everyone, we
know, you can't leave yet, says frederick, the crowd will thin, the
undesirables will leave, this is the problem, if there is one, my legs
carry me out, & nico wants to see the clean inside of my car, this

is a culture defining itself by what is not, this is the definition of want, make sure you get enough spit on it, make sure that flash of light isn't cops or headlights, if it's the sun coming up, that's ok, but it couldn't be, we'd never see it this deep in the district

love is finished again (2nd movement)

like if you stand in shadow & keep still
while the sun travels you will

once again be kissed by sun
or if you stand in a puddle the sun

will dry it
if you wait

& if you turn a right corner
four times you will come back

to the point where you began
finished

love
just like that

*

like opening a mirrored cabinet on your left
            & another mirror on your right to create

    the infiniti mirror effect

or like being penniless right before payday
            & then your bank balance rebounds

    love is finished like that

*

1 br garden apt, spectacular views

lights rushed & the constant whoosh
                    i missed _____
                                        & i missed red-white fences
                        beyond the highway that
                i called a writing studio

& in the room's windows raccoons
            climbed the trash bins
                        apple cores road kill the dirt

a fight i returned to the alcove
            the stove so clean it didn't start
                        something when i said use a covered pot
                as he got ready to sauté
tomato
                        i brought an armful of groceries tuna mayo
                            peanut butter
                                        a dill jar

& my lover
            he takes me he loves me
                        behind the deli counter
                                    a slippery sound on white vinyl
                        i've never been any such place

except w/him

                                    the once-intact bathroom
a third of it now painted white
                a third made of ripped wallpaper
                            & a garish bar mirror to cover the rest

take a tour & talk around the cottage
                                    i constantly think of leaving
                        i will invent a way

close my eyes & allow
            my face to be kissed pink & bare
                        he kneels beside my chair

in rain he'll come home feel sick turn green
                from the damp week i will
                                    have been gone
            he owns no new clothes his hair wet
                            in ripped white polo shirt
                        & thin denim jacket

a garden missing from it

the weekend goes quickly. driving home, I stop at a roadside bar.
I drink whiskey the color of wood paneling & tell the bartender
where I've been. but your grandmother died last summer, you just
said. my face goes white as linen when I remember my grandfather
died ten years before she did. then who did I just spend the
weekend with? I wonder, running for a payphone. I want to tell
my mother. & if what I've seen is possible, then maybe my first
love still lives in a basement room somewhere. with his unmade
bed & red coverlet. a handsome wooden storage chest rests at its
foot. a magazine open in front of him. one window lets in just
enough light to remind him of a world outside his little cell. maybe
it wasn't his body I saw pierced with medical tubes. his arm
shaking with effort to remove an oxygen mask. shaking with
urgency to tell me out loud, of course I recognize you.

while his husband is drinking in dallas

a belt, a pair of shoes, oil stain on the driveway,
these can be incriminating. someone drank mojitos &
danced merengue, hubby may think on sunday.
only we haven't. we just stand in the living room,

vaguely the middle, staring & daring each other. he
mentions a documentary. maps of brain waves music makes
in the minds of all animals. he shows me their shape
w/vigorous thrusting of hands, soon loses breath.

I almost finish his sentence. music is so
important, is all he can say. we agree there are things
more important. exhibit a. places he's never been.
I don't mean the moon, or the eye of a bulb, I mean

where his instincts have no meaning. he could be stranded
& sniffing the air for a fire. he knows who will come
to his rescue. who's to rescue me?
that's why I crave being outside my skin

& in someone else's. I sigh when I tell him this.
I use his first name w/certain intimacy. exhibit b.
earth doesn't care, & the sun's a waiting machine gun.
after the supernova they'll find me in the arizona desert

writing on backs of turtle shells about my dead aunt's
lipstick, a story I've been trying to tell for years.
this is when he turns on fans, the dishwasher, hairdryer,
television, all to distract my intention.

images move a mile a minute
across the screen. I talk about driving the highway they call
loneliest & suddenly realize I've seen him before, digging
in sand under rock on the side of the road, hiding

twelve months of the year in the only shade he finds.
twelve months of sun are like twelve months of snow
which reminds me of causes of sin. being good for too long,
you're bound to end up doing something wrong.

the spirit, I've learned, isn't much of anything except
perhaps an intersection. turn to him. let me
be clear. I want to move a mile a minute
under your thriving, pitching sun.

how to date everyone under the sun

when you wish to impress a pisces, draw one tarot card. let it
      be

page of cups. to ensnare an aries, wear your sailor's hat
      everywhere.

how to land a leo? with your leather jacket, tie both hands
      behind

your back. to make your cancer care, come with cotton-
      gauze-wrapped broken ribs.

to adore your virgo, think of the violin, how its scratchy
      throat

makes exquisite sounds. how to catch your taurus: chocolate
      covered cherries,

champagne in bed. how to love a libra? talk like a lawyer.
      make love

with witnesses present. to goose a gemini, two truths & a lie.

but if you play, don't let them win. to court your scorpio,
      tell secrets

not your own. show the dune beach where drowned bodies
      resurface. how to stir

sagittarius: in bed arrange silk threads belonging to no one

you know. to capture capricorn, flee papa razzi first-class.
      always

pay cash. how to acquire aquarius: send a message to reach
      him

when your ship vanishes on the horizon. let it be a moon
      song.

city boy hears crickets as advancing army sirens

I come to the mountain & listen. my mission, to find out what silence sounds like. I find it is not what you think. first you remove the whistling kettle to a cool burner. second ask the wind where it's come from in such a hurry. third you must wait for the rain to end. while it is singing you hear a whole bluegrass band, the picking of guitar strings, mandolins wailing behind moaning fiddles, almost like women in labor. you will swear you hear voices, a choir, but faintly. it may be the crickets, whose sound is like, when glass breaks, that shattering sound that's a series of tinier sounds. crickets are missing their collective noun, like cloud, the word for a group of grasshoppers. I will nominate one: a cotillion of crickets, after the rain stops, gossiping down by the creek. do you know, some birds stay awake all night? just like I do. door open. impossible to see apart tree bark black from black mountain rising into black sky. but now I know some things. silence is never still, it is motion, like when a mouth moves in a dream without a soundtrack. even when you subtract all the actions that spook & surprise & enliven you, you are left with what comes from within you. your pillow shushing the blood in one ear at time. like half a womb. or if you prefer, a faraway bomb.

in an average person's life
nations are warring 92% of the time

when our country goes into the gulf
with a war so short we call it a storm
my family goes to a new hampshire timeshare
when the tanks glow digital green on tv
& the bombs yellow-white mother turns on the jetsons
my younger brother & I share a bunkbed
we read from my favorite book about a squirrel
with glasses & a briefcase who solves mysteries

when young bush declares operation freedom
everyone in the college cafeteria hears war
including me I think of my brother
eighteen & weighing job options
the army always means free training stable pay
a solid career base & all our lives before this
it has never meant travel to hazard zones
to come eye to eye with weapons of mass

devastation between the two wars I am living
in california when every plane in america is
grounded that week a friend we grew up with drives
halfway to hartford where his college is
his car skids from the road the impact wastes

his body his weight a package of salt water
when I speak to his father on the phone
because I can't make the funeral I say his name

he says mine & we weep as though collapsed
in each other's arms we sit in this
comfort a moment but sometimes
I have this terrible thought that the dead
god forgive me are lucky in a way all the things
they didn't live to see & my brother has kids now
boys five & seven what will we say when they ask us
about the wreck that's coming & why we don't swerve

parade & ceremony

love is finished again (3rd movement)

like how your taxes pay
for another parade
& ceremony another fancy black tie gala

even when the politician's been
reelected to the same office

again love is finished

in its time & soon
every speech
ends

*

*

like when you lose your
        voice & it comes back

                        like sleep interrupted in dark
                hours when you know if you keep
        your eyes closed you'll return
to sleep & it to you

like a downhill slope of road
        is always followed by an uphill stretch
                though no two hills are alike

*

summers I would drive across america

green hill, black lake, peacock fireworks display i've never
        met a country
i didn't like a girl i meet for the first time every night every
noon on the footpath from woods someone hands us a klan
        meeting flyer
w/saddam hussein's photo on back is it true while we slept
        that our
army invaded turkey over a matter of pocket money?
is that real or did i make that up? like any good soldier that
        night
i say tell me you love me as barbara cartland has put it madly
the only person who gets my humor is my mother i turn to
my iphone, google sunset photos to see if this one's accurate
girl x & i stand on a cliff above folks singing the national
anthem, aching, baroque, & gorgeous why shouldn't they?
        i'm chewing gum
& watching her w/my one good eye follow her sisters in
        darkness
we slide down the slide with eyes closed, holding tight to
        each other the dense
forest plants have grown taller than us above us they lean in
        to kiss

my first kiss

she must've been the girl on the playground
who kissed all the boys
    & all the dogs too & cats the occasional
        turtle who served as classroom mascot

at sixteen she lost her virginity in the woods
by a brook & went to try to get it back
    in the arms of many more men
        in india ireland kenya new zealand

in the moment of giving herself she said
she loved every one of them in the moment
    of losing herself her kiss must've been
        a gift because maybe I was

a gay boy & we both knew or maybe
because I was hardest to kiss or maybe
    that kiss was a promise that I'd be the one
        to pick her up at airports the rest of our lives

draft divorce decree

every token I have given you shall remain
your property except the ring which let
the record show you refuse
to return / but I have its twin so
that's fine / & you retain ownership rights
to the world's furry bunnies & all woodland creatures
which remind me of you anyway // permission to trade
fathers is granted / our mothers' custody
will be handled jointly / I must have my ancestors'
burial site & the river
that borders it / & all the highways in america
were mine to begin with / & you
shall have all railway rights // you have
lay lake alabama with the cabin
& pontoon boat your parents own & gray trees
thick as an armory turret / but don't think
everything south of mason-dixon's yours because
virginia is for lovers & knoxville is the scruffy city
no one loves as I do // & as for all bicycle paths
we will have to work out
a signaling system / otherwise
we will collide & that
won't do while I train myself to believe
you are dead or never existed / not

walking these streets where I might walk
these brick sidewalks I've walked all my life // therefore
all of new england is mine / but you
have lifetime rights to reside
here / a sort of ground lease
granted to you this day by me / & you
can have montreal in summer if I
have the other three seasons / because
that's fair / amsterdam shall be yours but I
claim the right to visitation
exactly twice / all of the castles of europe
yours / except romantic france
shall be mine to roam / unless you're on a layover
or you pass through by rail // all islands of the world
are also yours because I
get seasick easily // remember
the drug you slipped me / that doubled
my vision & you
dimmed the light & kept watch? / next
day came the ring & I said
I would put my life in your hands again // which I did
when you drove the jet ski
at lay lake / where I return
whenever I dream a perfect place / in fact
when I find myself there //

that's precisely how I know that I am dreaming.

the night I asked you to break my heart

because the split we'd made was good for us both but this was two years later hope's long coma which could only end if the stronger of us pulled the cord from the power source so I packed my messenger bag with methods to rend my most important organ

steak knife hammer shards of broken mirror straitjacket guillotine in miniature & in case we needed something more powerful a magic book of curses

most spells are made w/words & broken by a kiss why not the other way around?

I'll spare everybody the bloody fine points of how we got it done & how I got home I can't remember but I lay a long time unable to sleep counting instead of sheep ex-loves who no longer take my calls

& in the event that they would take my calls I divided them like prison bricks into two piles

wouldn't know what to say & wouldn't know how to say it

as usual this left me spent & in sleep I dreamed seven dreams

I dreamed a helicopter in a hurricane it lifts but it'll never get anywhere

I dreamed the waiter saw I was thirsty but would not bring water

I dreamed my brother cut himself open with a scythe in my grandfather's garden

I dreamed I came to your birthday at the alabama governor's yellow mansion & no one turned to speak to me except your twin

I dreamed myself heaving up chunks of pink cupcake

I dreamed the world ended your way with a single glowing solar flare instead of my way & I dreamed my dead wrestled your dead

I say again my ghosts took up swords against your ghosts

& neither army had won when I twisted awake next morning but at least the strange man in my mirror wasn't as ugly as I remembered

the hardest part is knowing I'll survive

I see everything before it takes place
        my twin soul was a very old woman & while
        there is no perfect death I seek

a perfect setting for this death
        I know is coming whenever I take
        you back in my bed in the prairie
        in my arms in my mind you have said you prefer

a water burial what good is that to me
        who has marched in many a funeral on land
        where wind moves sand in circles like
        this talk of mine? do you even hear
        a thing asleep? I know your brand
        of pretend the sky you refuse
        the moon you refuse

tempted as I am to salt your wound
        you have no wound I can see
        I speak nattering nonsense seven seas
        several small seals
        little swift deaths ubiquitous
        none of my words ever trigger you

I observe death grow smaller each time
   I quit speaking & stay up late thinking
   the way any two -ing verbs rhyme
   is a cheat like the one we tried
   & the getaway failed the sound of me
   swept up & soon swallowed by other sound

I can not bear to look at cape cod light
   & let me not approach the causeway
   to the island of nahant I can't
   I won't though I am tired & you look peaceful
   when you imitate the dead in sleep while I
   cross people off lists & move to ever
   larger cities which is the custom
   of our ancestors who by the way bury
   themselves in earth I can't believe

how we leave the coffin in the end lonely
   adorned w/flowers that smell of fresh celery
   gunmetal cold in a chapel
   because we can't bear to see it
   cast a shadow & go finally into the ground

do not seek religion here

why? what's there to cry about.
                            firefly, fair sky, remote
like when I lived on the farm & one
of the girls fell down
                            the well? how dark. how did
                            he get his pants off? who could pass
through the gardens
where the feet were washed
                            the history of kisses
of betrayal, temptation
                            delivered. who would sashay
& not be stirred?
                            what's the opposite
of masturbation? a poem on porn
addiction? did I just say something
                            stupid? who did.
what are you doing waltzing
around with a chair. it can't
                            dance. & at your age.
blueberry crumble is today's special.
                            why am I here, flying
                            over a desert?
are we a long distance apart?
                            what's the opposite of art.

adventure?—are they brothers? lovers?
                                      & did that hand know
what the other was doing? neither cares
                                      who you're screwing
at what hour.   voices—how many? have I
broken the law? why not
                                      open the jaw with an oar
& clean out the clock &
                                      find out. you know how. is it all
done with mirrors? it's clear we're
obsessed—who isn't.   can you tell me
                                      where the flocks are?
did he have to tell them,
pointing the way to heaven
                                      like philippe petit on wire
between his towers?

how freedom feels under an authoritarian regime

THURSDAY | news scroll says a mime in black w/green beret
    dangles from the eiffel tower observation deck
    I assume this is a failed romantic gesture
    someone's pouring gasoline along the tower's base

SATURDAY | my lover has tied my wrists & I wear a blind
    for thirteen years I trained my eyes to see in the dark
    by keeping awake lying still as a coma in the basement
    when no one was home the only sound a refrigerator
        motor

MONDAY | I pay a sicilian witch who refuses to make curses
    & she draws a prince of swords for me
    when she leaves we make love again while a swarm of bees
    panic themselves against the window screen

WEDNESDAY | I've been planning to ask my darling to marry
    & maybe should've kept planning instead of say why
    don't we do it this weekend? he says I should return
    to writing poetry & goes & shaves off all his ass hair

TUESDAY | remember the automobile a symbol of american
    ideals wealth freedom speed & coolness & heat &

while furniture shopping I have a premonition my car
will have a flat tire when I leave the store

SUNDAY | always more on the news scroll drowned bodies
    lined up along the dirty shore but sometimes I wake up
    to pastry hot coffee & ocean smell but I worry about baby
    turtles & why has my lover been gone from this scene so
        long?

FRIDAY | leather jacket & sixty five chevy & if this
    were prom night we'd be in a familiar film maybe made
    when my mom was a teen & remade for my generation
    I know where there's train tracks to dance with so let's jet

    & let this be the last drive we ever fucking take

love is finished again (4th movement)

once you cross a border you can
in fact cross back again but
you can never un-cross

*

unrequited fuckboy

the way I love you is only possible
because I know next to nothing
about you boy from the neighborhood
I know your eyes that look as if
you wear permanent eyeliner I love the lashes
that protect them & could swat a fly from
across the sunroom I know your rules like
condoms no exceptions while we make love I insist
you look deep in my eyes & if you force me
to insist one more time I may playfully
slap your cheek while I whisper
what is more intimate than a whisper? what is
the real reason you can't love me back?
is it your white collar family
w/their sailboat in the bay & summers
on the island? is it because I prefer the taste
of artificial coconut to your unsweet earth safe
organic water? mumbler your mouth barely opens
whenever you speak will you never
make clear declarations? will all conversations
be bedroom conversations after I render you
too tired to leave? but you do leave
whenever I suggest you stay will you never stay
from first whiskey until next day? will I never

write an aubade? a poem for lovers who
part at dawn? the only poem I know how to write is
the aubade's opposite a fragment
of two queers cruising after midnight

loving all these men. is that what I think

I've been doing? honey, if I'm real,
I been fuckin' around. & when did I insist
on ruining myself? like someone who ruins

a shirt in a bike wreck. ok, there are many
more ways to ruin. skinned knees, blood & dirt
are the basics. to ruin is to spoil. think of fruit

spilled in wind. it disintegrates slowly, its rind
resembling, for a long time, a shell. this also
happens to bodies left on the farm unburied.

to ruin is to leave ruins, noseless busts,
torn porcelain faces, shards of columns,
caves of pompeii with angels frescoed

on walls of what were surely brothel rooms.
what I want is to get the root of one person's
ruin by their own hand. the way my car's been dented

on every side: once from my bike collapsing
against a door, once when I backed up hard
into carolina bedrock, once when a snowplow

chewed the forward wheel well. that summer,
my front bumper snagged on a pole & tore,
metal shrieked as I pulled away after midnight

from the man who panted with me smoke-hot, quiet
breaths at the head of his driveway. he didn't want
to wake his husband sleeping in the vinyl-sided house.

career planning for young poets

darling when we were nineteen the question
what do you do had no answer
& you went away to india to dig
maggots from forgotten street dogs'

wounds before they rotted I stayed home
to see about a job & got to see american
pie the weekend it came out I stayed & opened
my first credit card & bought a bus ticket

for rome new york for woodstock '99
you got used to mud & learned to kill
chickens & I went for the music ok
I went for the first boy I didn't know I loved

who loved alt rock ok ok I did it for that monster
truck guitar hook from that damn good song
my own worst enemy we couldn't know
generals somewhere smoked fat cigars &

planned wars for your men to go fight
I figured if I bragged of my first blow
job I myself could sidestep combat I consumed
as my patriotic duty ok I ate for comfort & got

an eating disorder I stayed home so someone could
say hi to your parents whenever
I swam in their green pool at night
nothing was certain except it would kill us

to become them I was boring & thought you
a hypocrite who loved every place you went & cared
nothing for people because they can't love
the planet & your gods the animals & trees

& I only felt free when I bought my first car
loan our love then not so much fragile as
untested & now the world sees me richer
than you I own a piece of rock in the city's

cross-hatched lots & you work clearing trails
I pay my taxes & deduct my debt
I separate my waste & compost bones
& seeds & try to take the stairs

my bicycle rusts & I write in my head
en route to the office & sweetie I can't even drive
my hybrid to the country to see you without
stopping off the highway to buy latte & a scone

love is finished again (5th movement)

        like a batch of biscuits
burned & you have to start
        baking all over again
or like a many layered cake
        with alternating flavors
raspberry lemon vanilla repeat
        love is just like that
have you ever noticed it?

*

*

like the mailbox w/paper stuffed in it but

some days it is empty

eventually it will fill again

*

body & literary

yrs,

how randall signs his emails
taken literally means he's mine dear randall i miss you

too bud & nights at the writers retreat
we talked booze & drank big ideas & i'm

grateful to read yr new poem i love
how summer dies like an old loyal hound

so sorry to hear ur alone at the farm
how long will yr wife be gone?

dear diary i rly think if i drive south
to his humid house w/whiskey in hand he'd

open the door & let me suggest
some fun drinking game played with a blindfold

he'd let me see him
naked & i'd finally get to rub his fuzzy belly

dear gods of desire what is it about gazing on a man
so handsome it almost hurts

to look? the little-boy quality
in his voice? how he hangs on my words asking

how i know what i know?

dear therapist doesn't it say in yr notes
i never chase straights? nevermind toxic masc

& fragility panic it takes so much energy to land
a play date w/someone who likes licking dick

& sometimes a guy rubs against me & my mind
just attaches to sadness at that moment

a mud-splattered truck screeches up to the stop sign
& I hear twang twang of country guitars

dear randall i don't rly like
dark liquor but bourbon it shall be

unless by chance you want as i want
you sober open-eyed longing pouring from yr mouth

into mine like a slow gush of spit

o muses i see now why all gays before me wrote
poems & made stage plays

dear self we are always honest with each other
        tonight i want to smell what randall's

    insides smell like not another night
of porn & nail polish remover to prolong

        my pleasure past my own
    weak wrist so let's get some shoes on

repeat after me
    phone wallet keys

possession diary

after Marie Howe

the 1st devil was my craving for salty snacks.

2nd, a habit of dashing off emails in anger. a twenty-four-hour cooldown period is always advisable.

3rd, I could see the future.

4th place, I could never decide how I felt about procreation.

5th was not a specific song, but the fact that melody never left my mind. I was always hearing music, even when I wasn't listening to it. whistling something or other. or sometimes holding my lips in the shape of a whistle but sucking in air, a shrill imitation of wind. in my head, fat brass, soaring strings, chiming bells, the whole bit.

ok the 1st was I would eat anything put in front of me, just because it was there.

the 2nd was how I always believe I'm right. not simply in matters of fact, but emotionally right. right to love this person or hate that one, even when compelling evidence says I should not, & that belief in my rightness leads to righteous anger, that skin-burn from a hot stove.

3rd was I thought I had reversed the aging process.

4th was my fear that the worm which fed on my father's brain for twenty-seven years also lives in me. that a loud enough pop, as from a balloon, might waken it & make it hungry.

5th was I too much enjoyed the smells of my own body. the smells of my body had their own melody.

6th was I could not love ordinary men, only wolves or their hunters, canine packs.

7th, severe halitosis. no doctor, chemical, prayer, or spell could cure me. as a child, I went to school w/dead fish breath & my hair always sticking up, even if I had combed it & brushed my teeth. finally I learned to cut all my hair off.

there was no comparable solution for my tongue.

maybe that was my 1st & original devil.

the 2nd was that patience eluded me. children try to chase the moon, but it never gets any closer. I wished for patience like the ocean wishes to be less restless.

the 3rd was that I knew things, like: that it took eight minutes to walk to the train stop, which meant I needed to leave my bed at 7:50, which meant the latest I should ever go to sleep was 1:05.

ok. the 1st was I ate so quickly I bit the inside of my mouth. when the soft scar was still healing, I'd bite there again. that happened so many times.

the 2nd was I blatantly disregarded stop signs inside parking lots.

3rd was that I believed nothing ever happened, nothing could, exactly the way I imagined it. in this way, I prevented many disasters & a few happy outcomes.

4th was I was a chronic masturbator.

5th was that I could have been a great actor, but I got stage fright as a five-year-old playing the wizard in the wizard of oz. I spent all the rest of my days trying to be invisible.

6th was martyr syndrome, also known as doormat disease, which I inherited from my mother. people who make themselves doormats, especially for their mates, I considered angels. also I believed in the virtue of living in poverty. stupid, stupid.

7th was indulgence. I never masturbated in my grandparents' house, until one day I felt it would kill me to wait. that day forward I let myself do it there, but only in the basement bathroom.

everything in my life was like this. a want that became a need. a bad thing that became a habit, until I couldn't distinguish right from wrong.

the truth is there were many more than seven devils. the truth is I ordered them a car. I cleaned my body while they drove to meet me. I placed a mirror by my bed, hid my wallet, unlocked the door, & let them do whatever, whatever, whatever they wanted to me.

the invention of sex

IT MAY HAVE HAPPENED this way: flight delays, one husband's return from a business trip, he fears quick death in the rear of a yellowcab which slides across six lanes & speeds up the avenue of the americas. finally he attains home & finds his husband asleep, husband number two having wished & prayed eight days for this return, having washed where he knows husband one wants to kiss hello, 'I am back, did you miss this?,' having unwillingly fallen asleep like a relative in a surgical waiting room. in case this description of husband one & two is awkward, let's call them instead 'business body' & 'librarian body.' or let's call them 'physical body' & 'literary body.' one body at rest & one body in motion as I undress in the dark & slide into place, draped not by the blanket but by the flanks of my lover. his body smells naturally clean, like moss after rain, & his mouth tastes of beer, & he says my mouth's a dirty martini. maybe he speaks from inside a dream. IT MUST HAVE HAPPENED this way: we the inventors, we, not the cavemen. one hand naturally forms the shape of an 'o' during sleep, & two sleeping bodies are usually no more than two-thirds asleep. that's plausible, right? but we gladly recall these cavemen: we ritually dance around a fire, we shake & flash our burning sticks like man-shaped peacocks, we groove like shakers under a mirror ball, our grunted songs an aria of ecstasy, until a whole village joins in.

the best don't have to brag (but they still do)

it started with a swagger line

      the best thing that happened to sex
      since the devil invented it

cuz i seen my dick become
the devil's pitchfork

that's fucking confidence

you know when sometimes
you know you dangerous?

        every damn day
        is devil-dangerous but me i'm doing poetry
        a favor

      the english language gonna thank me
      when I'm done
      whoring it out

      my proverbs instant proverbs
      my lyrics tomorrow's
      trending clichés

you heard me right

soon as i'm done w/this poem they'll be
memorializing me

        they won't even wait

like the subway dancers passing the hat said

        your money is never obligated
        but i ain't doing this for free

interview after accepting big literary award

after Pasolini

I on the cross & he on the couch 'you sir' with his nails
     I know what he thinks what he sees
   'so much recent success as a writer!' licks his lips
        'maybe the next ryan murphy?'

      HISSSS! he cobra in turquoise warby parkers
   & me foaming magnesium white in silence
he clears his throat 'remind me &
      our readers what you're working on?'

      POEMS 'I write poems!' & you KNOW that
    cursed creature whose mother's milk
   must've been sour 'poems no longer
     in tercets!' a joke he doesn't get
    don't you see? this is key! no longer in tercets!
'I've returned to the primordial stew
    of collective unconscious the anima mundi' I mean to say
      capitalism is ending baby & we've won
   though I live on the sidewalk & do haiku
for pocket change in a subway station &
     hjs for bitcoin till I can land a job
      at a government run university

& this snake bitch with his sharp pen 'what's
               the title of your next book?' 'I don't know…'
          oh now he wants me to perform
smile little monkey 'maybe The Persecution:
     A New History' something like that I wish
               I were squeezing my mother's deathbed hand
or anywhere else 'of the Hebrew People'

                    WHY would I say that? conversation fails
          w/the energy of an extra feminine syllable
inging at the end of an amateur sonnet
          primordial stew?! who even am I now? 'interesting
                         this is about?' your death
                    your murder by body
          blow from this goddamn chair 'you see we poets
               live w/this constant risk of not communicating
          not being comprehended…' if the cobra could
     know that even this statement is not my
               original thought 'they are nearly all lyric poems
     situating different subjects in time & space'

               say panoramas pastorals! say petit four
                    puit d'amour!
something that sounds beautiful intelligent
          say monuments maleness whiteness say we all ride
the same commuter cars 'haha' interjects king cobra

with his nasty pen 'who is it that
            doesn't understand?' 'I think I need
                        a glass of water' this is not hell it is real
life & therefore will be over soon

half hour later 'therefore according to
                        you' he makes a hesitant start he chews
            at last his pen 'what in fact is the definition
of social justice?' & w/that
            he leans forward about to take notes

love is finished again (6th movement)

like one violin   that cries a string of notes
is always joined by   a partner violin
extending the cry   while one violin
takes a break   to breathe
the wind comes   off the strings
as off a body   of water
love is finished   love begins
taking over from   another love

*

resurrection spell

begin with a spiral mountain road with no end, its curves a
familiar, smooth drive. one morning my mind is composing a
theory of body as more than bone, as a series of rooms configured
vertically, all hung together by bakery string. seeing only a stick, I
roll my tires neatly over what becomes a black snake. fact: black
snakes are harmless. what's the mathematics of surface area
pressure? what is the weight of this car? last night on a rainforest
walk, an unseen black bird took flight. abruptly shoved off his
thick green cover to flee. my body's response? blood fear, a
chemical reminder I'm animal first. my mother's mother sat at the
bedside of great-grandma camilla & knew the hour she'd die.
camilla tried to leave her bed, pleading, needing to touch feet to
ground one more time. this woman in a hospital bed did not mean
tile, she meant black soil. & I spend hours conjuring my first love,
charming him back from the dead with words he left me. I could
touch his black hair again while he smiles with bloodshot eyes.
when last I saw him, his body was simply slack weight, a deflated
membrane his mother would sponge-wash. fact: a snake run over
slithers back into the greenery soundlessly, not even curling its
tongue. fact: its vertebrae are cracked, its ribs are crushed, its injury
will be lethal, but not right away. I'll still be driving home, radio
loud, raising songs that bring my baby alive. a snake in this kind of
pain takes a long time with its dying.

[auto-reply text message]
the poet is driving right now

I can still see you
tomorrow night and maybe
next weekend I wanna

thanks for the woof handsome
guy for you doing
everything well I'll be sure
to give him some

hugs. hi there are we
gonna do it tomorrow or tomorrow
morning or maybe I should go?

I don't think I ever
got to be this way
until the end
of my life lol

self-talk in end times

what's your inner voice like? is it
angry with commands? quit

talkin' about this wound as if it never
closed. stop talkin' about war as if it never

was. do you kiss your favorite pet
or your mother with that mouth? oh, forget

it, you can't, you're an orphan since age three.
is that the story

you want to stick to? what do you feel
every time you sit behind the wheel,

what's the word for a brain stuck
like a jeep's turn signal you're behind in fuck-

ing traffic, blinking, blinking, & you itch to turn left.
a parking lot is where you sat when he left

& you can't say his name, not in this poem,
but it showed up on street signs, billboards, comm-

ercials, awnings above every general store
for years (how many? you don't count anymore.)

& what about the so-called
world beyond the self? remember your bald

boss used to say 'the problem with your generation
is, you never had a war or a recession.'

like magic, you suffered both, worse than his age ever
had it. what a coincidence that war's the best cure

for depressions (economic). you've been water-boarded, but
you can't confess, your tongue's been cut

out. you can't name catastrophe,
ashy skies & iceberg oceans caused by the orgy

of war. some territory's too big to explore
today. you only got two legs & worn out footwear.

so stay here, navel-gazing, eating like it's a holiday, buying
like it's going out of style. whining,

feed me, love me. if you say 'the end'
& no one's here to take pics, did it really happen?

a gen xer & a millennial speak on the end of the world

when you've just finished reading apocalypse
novels & your slightly younger boyfriend's
addicted to climate change
articles & you have faith that what's
coming whether zombie virus h1n1
solar flare whatever happens first
doesn't matter you'd rather imagine
what kind of wagon you'll escape on
you & your love when that late afternoon
light disturbs some future morning
but he says phytoplankton have begun
to smother like goldfish gasping
on kitchen counters & coral reef
will soon be only museum relics
& he argues whether bernie
can still win you interrupt
to list a few artful approaches
you've seen in the literature but then
the razor in his voice when he says
I'll stop talking I'll just listen
between gritted teeth firmly
as if you've raised a fist
then you find your lip quivers

with the tension of a dam & did I mention
you are riding the red line when the crying
begins? you both get out at harvard square the acrid
summer garbage smell welcomes you but isn't
what's stinging your eyes that now drizzle
like the cake ace on food network
& he apologizes honey honey
honey for the nothing wrong he did
& by the time you get to elephant & castle
you don't feel like eating
the host who seats you didn't want to come
to work tonight & your weeping
doesn't help & everyone in the restaurant
wonders if your date attacked you
or if your parents have cancer so you go
to the basement & find a urinal still leaking
from your eyes & stare at a poster of red
double-decker buses in london & that should cheer
you up so you start talking
to yourself in a british accent
because sometimes you don't have a bloody clue
why the bollocks you're still crying

colossus endowed

I too have savored the phrase five o'clock shadow in my
      mouth
like the hidden key to my diary
I have always known masculinity was money
was the currency that makes the world turn
it's like this: certain currents flow but to cross an ocean takes
      an engine

or at least an oar & one good arm
in other words muscle
musk is older boys who led expeditions in the woods & did
      things
like throw & tackle fish & swim
they were earning early wages accruing interest while I

shy geisha w/passive male gaze would quietly create
my pen forgot nothing
what the bathing suit outlined
the patch of hair above the tan lines no detail too tiny
o masculinity masc we all wear

there were days I'd count hairs that sprouted under my arm
a razor came to shear my upper lip & level my sideburns
& now I am grown & a man calls before a first date

to check if I possess a loose letter s or singsong vowels
that would mark me lower class I don't like

when a man w/chiseled cheekbones says hey you could
        basically pass as straight
I resent when a younger man sees my bush & salivates
says o daddy & places me in his safe deposit box
what if I want to flip over & be plowed clean & held?
if I speak of a mutual equal dynamic forget it may as well call
        a rideshare

& when do we drop the masc & embrace depravity? what
if what I want is a power otter to be my owner for a while?
masc makes envy & enemies anyone can see who has it &
        who doesn't
omnipresent it is gravity
omnipotent it is god

fuckboy (second night)

I was aware I was wholly ridiculous
(see also lovefool) when I thought
the word (love) & declared to myself
(no better word) & with our quick telepathy

asked (if you had the mortal courage
to claim love) I hit your prostate
hard then (fear widened your eyes) & you said
(I love you) & I understood

(one) that one definition of love is
to hear this idea (as a sentence in the mind)
two (I fell in love) as I was writing this
poem (& also forgetting your name)

which is one measure of (how much
I love you) & three although you moan my name (to call
me back to earth) I can't tear myself (out
of the love poem) which is another

measure of how much (I love you) & four
I have been loving you thus that I forget
to eat (now I am fed by some other means)
& fifth with your powers I know you can lift

(can levitate me) from the bed (as in
an exorcism) pitch me down in a black swath of hell (& it
will be the real hell) & the name I scream
to damn will be your name (if I remember

in that thrill of pain) & I'll never murder
for you (but I will inflict pain) more pain
on your body (than any other body)
& despite this fistful of proofs I'm aware (the ugly truth

remains) I haven't solved the riddle
of love (& I hope I'll die with it
unsolved) here where you witness life bleed (from
this vigorous) given to me only briefly body

sound & gesture

love is a temple love the higher law

like an unwashed tongue the road rolls

toward me & away at seventy mph I'm giving
    a concert at top volume a magnitude of blood
        crawls in my temples & leadens my head

bowed low with new weight though my back
    has been hunched in a sob seven years & my bowels
        shake because I have taken the dense blue pill

which will eat the virus if it managed to breach
    my skin last time I pulled a man down in my lap
        to feel my love inside out like the bee gees sang

in sex ed I paid attention on disease day they said it is
    smaller than any bacterium now every time I swallow
        my own saliva I wonder is my swallow normal or
            inflamed

if no infection but glands swollen it could be the flu
    that warns new converts with hiv six weeks after it starts
        making as many molecular copies as the body has
            cells

there is no way the human mind can visualize a trillion
    this dark lullaby also vibrated in my ears the day
        at fifteen I left the house the yard the family like

a stray electron broke free from its compound I was young
    but I knew how a man demolishes his wife or children
        or self-destructs pointing at his head before he

raises the wrecking ball or hammer or shotgun slug O
    love O god O man I'm gonna come
        a distance greater than any ache

carrying in this body one infection
    to give you with my love I know you can taste
        how I decided that day to go on living as long as

I could & yet the male ejaculate on skin
    is the cleanest smell there is
        it is the closest thing

a man alone can make to a newborn child

love is finished again (7th movement)

once you have been born to one
father you can't be
un-born or be born to another

you can only scream
& cry & hope they feed
you & bring you

someplace safe & eventually
you rock
yourself to sleep

*

kiss my lisp

three times monthly speech therapy in my youth.
therapist seth assured my growth,
though I questioned his ethics. synth

thrummed my walls. pathologized, I wore teen goth,
thief of milky skin & mascara eyes beneath
thorny hair lacquered black. a wraith,

thin lips wrapped around smokes. a birthday, my 16th—
then, I think, first trip to the video booth.

there was seth,

thick-necked, 23—I know—but this was leavenworth,
threadbare military town. he taught my mouth
think of that consonant that clings to teeth,

throat his length, which I did with
thirsty technique. & now if you think me uncouth,
thank you. & thank him. I know my worth.

therapy isn't how I learned we're all from one doomed earth.

that night & a trip to barcelona in 11th,
they fostered new interests—muscles, girth,
threesomes, absinthe. musical depth,

theory & romance mingled. beethoven's 9th
theme, ode to joy. life was mirth.
thrive I could, did, shall, & so forth.

we never spoke of dodge city again

if we woke some nights tangled in blankets
in a white & black room I knew it meant we'd fallen

asleep again before a movie ended
mornings I'd roll over & look

at the mirror rather than at him
I did not know the hazel eyes would fade

faster than someone's scent from a shirt sleeve
or pillowcase there were exactly five theories

of love at the time according to my notebook
no tests for those theories you just had to know

months later we drove from one coast
to another & not the same city

passenger & driver whatever else we were
by the time we reached kansas

we were its ghost a wisp of smoke
lit by the red glare of tail lights

nearly invisible dust hovering over a mound of dirt
what little skin we had

dried up in wind in small towns with white water towers
where orphaned branches blew along the ground

outside of squat brick houses somewhere before junction city
he paused to show me the millions of stars

I had never looked at them before never strained
my body looking stretched all my senses

as if to trap galaxies tightly inside me
I knew their light would die before we arrived

the sudden lack of atmosphere astounded me & he
flew from my limbs so thin & airy that I barely noticed

there was one bridge in kansas
we crossed it

when I fall in love, I don't say

I'm in love. I say I'm in trouble.
the way I love is any joni mitchell song,
a wild silk beauty, dark & unexplainable,

a jazz in seven registers, vulnerable.
the body's most sensitive place is tip of tongue.
I'm in love, I say. I'm in trouble

when his mood & moon wane, inevitable.
after feeling, men get alone & want nothing,
their wild slick beauty dark & unattainable.

the way they love is opposite-double,
wave-particle theory. I always get it wrong
in love. I say I'm in trouble,

hearing the omen drumbeat. I tremble
before the coming movement, crescendo, clang,
a weird trick, beauty dark & inescapable.

before I bled with love, words were mere symbols
of the real. a gray thing, biteless, with no sting.
I'm in love, I say. I'm in trouble,
a world-sick body, dumb & inconsolable.

wouldn't it be better if you could just come over?

I don't know how to get it
      get it going right before I get home
I get home and get some
      errands done & then
& then we can do dinner
      dinner was great but the worst
part was the best
      the best way is to be the most
handsome guy ever
      ever see a pic of that guy
that knows how to get it?
      get it out of my mind
my mind was thinking about
      you doing something nice (thumbs-up emoji)
morning was fun but wasn't it too late?
      too late for the night
the night the party
      the weekend the trip

let's catch up soon

awesome thanks man how's it gonna go
because it was just too much
can I see the snow tomorrow morning
did I tell you that I don't want to see
everything else I have is going going
fun game to pass the time and fun to watch
great how are they doing good job haha
haha is my dad I gotta get going
it going haha I am just getting home now
job interview with a good friend of yours
keep it up and I'll let it all out again
love it going on my list
maybe I'll try something else to make sure
nice app but it's not really nice
oh wow let me know guys when we find something to say
probly not too late to get there and then I'll probly go home
question forgot to ask if I wanna do the time
right now I'm sorry to bother you but I'll be sure to check in
sorry to hear about your dad|trip|friend
that's great how about yourself and how much fun
ugh I'm going to try on my own now
visiting with friends today and this took about a month
well that's cool (sunglasses emoji) I'll be in the shower
xactly what I'm saying it is true and I appreciate that

yes I'm sure they were just lying but it wasn't right
zero chance of that

black & white study with lover
framed in a church door

this is your first performance art.

after the guggenheim a church with its pews.

removed its balconies.

lined with lights a bare altar.

floor like a gymnasium polished light wood.

we roam the anterooms.

one room with laundry one.

with piano & dancing girl.

we branch in our separate directions until.

I stand in one corner & notice.

you in the opposite corner returning.

into the main room there could not be.

more distance than this between us.

I see your whole body & realize.

I have never.

seen you walk before.

the night I first meet you I pace between five.

horse tavern & the davis square t stop.

thinking I've missed you but then.

you are there.

your beard bathed in light from a closed laundromat.

closer than in this church this night.

I am used to seeing your eyes up close.

staring up at mine or closed.

on the pillow or looking at my chest.

& smiling.

brow worried as you fill.

with delight as I fill you.

or I have watched you walk from behind.

the pockets of your gay jeans are too low.

as you know.

another night you are so hard.

in the car I have to pull over.

& put my mouth on you.

& you ask is it safe.

& the answer is yes.

because we are in darkness.

the city's paradox.

900 cars pass by.

while the mamas & the papas sing.

monday monday while I make.

you in the passenger seat.

achieve pleasure you need.

I do not know or care.

if you have ever done that before.

this time is ours & tonight.

is brightly lit.

a performer rolls in her rug-like pajamas.

toward me & away from you.

like a roly poly bug & digging.

this scene you follow.
her & take.
her picture.
I give myself an assignment.
to describe this kind of light.
& know it will take years.
fine.
let it take twelve years.
let them be the agonizing years.
of my life let my beard grow white.
& let it be the most perfect.
new york poem.
I ever write.

enough

I'm not a new yorker but I can walk
like one & one warm night I cross 8th ave
at 14th street which is rufus wainwright's
best song (but don't let that major key

big brass & broadway piano fool you
when someone hurls your heart like a potted plant
from the roof of a ten-story building
you will feel all your organs shrivel) & I happen to

raise my head in time to see emerge
from the subway station below two latino men
older than I am 50 maybe turn to each other
& say 'love you' & press their wet lips together in

that sound & gesture in swedish *puss-puss*
the men part in different directions & relief
straightens my back & I think for this rare minute
there is enough love in the world.

Notes

The sestina "wallflower's complaint" takes its end terms from the Michael Jackson song "Billie Jean."

"love is finished again" is inspired by the Yehuda Amichai poem of the same title, as translated by Chana Bloch and Stephen Mitchell in *The Selected Poetry of Yehuda Amichai*, University of California Press, 1996.

"a letter to my therapist while I am high" is inspired by and references brief text from the James Baldwin novel *Giovanni's Room*.

"the whatever store on route 111" (not a real place) is inspired by a prompt from poet and memoirist Brian Turner.

"21st century love song" is a cento with lines borrowed from the following sources: Song of Songs, The Bible (public domain); Rihanna, "We Found Love," 2011; Ellie Goulding, "Love Me Like You Do" (from *Fifty Shades of Grey*), 2015; Madonna, "Love Profusion," 2003; Beyonce and Jay-Z, "Crazy in Love," 2003; Maroon Five, "Never Gonna Leave This Bed," 2010; Diamond Rings, "Runaway Love," 2012; Sondre Lerche, "To Be Surprised" (from *Dan in Real Life*), 2007; Shelby Lynne, "Killin' Kind" (from *Bridget Jones's Diary*), 2001; Tanya Donnelly, "The Night You Saved My Life," 2002; Dashboard Confessional, "Stolen," 2006; Joss Stone, "Put Your Hands on Me," 2006; Jason Mraz,

"I'm Yours," 2008; Bobby Bare Jr., "Your Adorable Beast," 2004; Katy Perry, "Teenage Dream," 2010; Jennifer Hudson, "Love You I Do" (from *Dreamgirls*), 2006; Cee Lo Green, "I Want You," 2010; The Vaccines, "I Always Knew," 2012; Keri Wilson with Kayne West and Ne-Yo, "Knocks You Down," 2009; Madonna, "Don't Tell Me," 2000; The Magnetic Fields, "If There's Such a Thing As Love," 2004.

"while listening to 'the young person's guide to the orchestra'" is inspired by the recording of Benjamin Britten's "Variations and Fugue on a Theme of Purcell" as used in the recording "The Young Person's Guide to the Orchestra" by Leonard Bernstein, which appears on the soundtrack and in the film of Wes Anderson's *Moonrise Kingdom*.

"the violent bear it *spoiler alert **trigger warning" refers to Flannery O'Connor's novel *The Violent Bear It Away*, whose title in turn comes from the Bible. The last lines refer to the poem "Clean Slate" by Sharif Shanahan, from *Into Each Room We Enter Without Knowing*, Southern Illinois University Press/Crab Orchard Series in Poetry, 2017.

"hi-nrg edm & me" was inspired by a warehouse party in Brooklyn, and I learned the term "hi-nrg edm" from DJ Jeffrey Sfire's bio.

"1 br garden apt, spectacular views" uses a three-term list written by Rousz DeLuca.

"how to date everyone under the sun" and "summers I would drive across america" are written in an American Sonnet form innovated by Diane Seuss. The Barbara Cartland reference in "summers" plays on Umberto Eco's explanation of postmodernism in *Postscript to The Name of the Rose*, Harcourt Brace Jovanovich, 1984.

"in an average person's life nations are warring 92% of the time" is a false fact deduced from true facts in the first chapter of *What Every Person Should Know About War* by Chris Hedges, Simon & Schuster, 2003, reprinted in *The New York Times* July 6, 2003.

"the hardest part is knowing I'll survive" is a line from the Emmylou Harris song "Boulder to Birmingham," 1975, whose lyrics inspired this poem.

"do not seek religion here" repeats questions asked in Lloyd Schwartz's *Cairo Traffic*, The University of Chicago Press, 2000.

"possession diary" takes its form and inspiration from the poem "Magdalene—The Seven Devils" by Marie Howe.

"interview after accepting big literary award" is an adaptation of lines from the Pier Paolo Pasolini poem "Una Disperata Vitalitá," or "A Desperate Vitality," parts II and IV, available in English in *Pier Paolo Pasolini: Poems*, selected and translated by Norman MacAfee with Luciano Martinengo, from Farrar, Straus and Giroux, 1996.

"resurrection spell" is dedicated to kurt g. hall (1968-2013), whose emails inspired the madness in this poem.

"[auto-reply text message] the poet is driving right now," "wouldn't wouldn't it be better if you could just come over?" and "let's catch up soon" were written with the assistance of Apple's predictive text function. Each word represents a choice I made from three choices presented by the Apple robot.

"colossus endowed" was inspired by the Sylvia Plath poem "The Colossus" and a prompt from poet Tyler Allen Penny, who also inspired "self-talk in end times."

"love is a temple love the higher law": Title and several words come from the U2 song "One."

"black & white study with lover framed in a church door" refers to a series of performances organized and presented by Danspace Project in 2016.

"enough" references the Rufus Wainwright song "14th Street" from the 2003 album *Want One*.

Acknowledgments

Thanks to the editors of the following journals in which some of these poems, or earlier versions of these poems, first appeared.

"when I was an uber driver," first appeared in *Puerto del Sol*.

"who do you think you are?" appeared in *2 Bridges Review*.

"love is finished again" appeared in its entirety in *Breakwater Review*.

A version of "a letter to my therapist while I am high" was published in *Stirring*.

"hi-nrg edm & me" and "the invention of sex" appeared in the anthology *Pan's Ex: Queer Sex Poetry* from Qommunicate Publishing, 2019.

"a garden missing from it" was first printed in *descant*.

"while his husband is drinking in dallas" was published in *Cider Press Review*.

"city boy hears crickets as advancing army sirens" appeared in *Jet Fuel Review*.

"draft divorce decree" appeared in *Poet Lore*.

"the night I asked you to break my heart" appeared in *Crab Fat Magazine*.

"the hardest part is knowing I'll survive" was printed in *The Florida Review*.

"do not seek religion here" first appeared in *Water Stone Review*.

"loving all these men. is that what I think" was published in *West Trade Review*.

"yrs," appeared in *Scoundrel Time*.

"possession diary" was first runner-up in *Storm Cellar*'s 2019 Force Majeure Flash Contest and appeared in the publication in 2020.

"resurrection spell" was published in *Arkana* and won its Editor's Choice Award.

"[auto-reply text message] the poet is driving right now" and "wouldn't it be better if you could just come over?" appeared in *Summerset Review*.

"self-talk in end times" was published in *Monday Night*.

"a gen xer and a millennial speak on the end of the world" appeared at *Califragile*.

"kiss my lisp" first appeared in *Jabberwock*.

"we never spoke of dodge city again" appeared in *Assaracus*.

"love is a temple love the higher law" was first published in *Washington Square Review*.

"when I fall in love, I don't say" was printed in *Connecticut River Review*.

"let's catch up soon" appeared in *The Southampton Review*.

"enough" was published in *Ocean State Review*.

Special thanks to the following organizations that provided scholarships and time and space for these poems to be written and revised: Azule in Hot Springs, North Carolina; Stony Brook University in Stony Brook and Southampton, New York; and Sundress Academy for the Arts in Knoxville, Tennessee.

Thank you to these readers, peers, and mentors who were instrumental in my writing and revision process for these poems in particular: Claudia Acevedo-Quiñones, Miranda Beeson, Laure-Anne Bosselaar, Jericho Brown, Rousz DeLuca, Amy Hempel, sam sax, Diane Seuss, Julie Sheehan, and Terese Svoboda.

To the amazing writers from my MFA cohort who continue to support me, surprise me, and always have my back: thanks and love to you all, especially Miranda Beeson, Rousz DeLuca, Tyler Allen Penny, Lily Wann, and of course my Writers Cottage roommates/sisters Natalie De Paz and Zinnia Owen Smith. And special thanks & love to the writer and artist who has been there since the beginning, believing we could do this, Kris Ringman.

I am indebted to Walt Odets for his first book *Out of the Shadows: Reimagining Gay Men's Lives*, which gave me the courage and audacity needed to complete this project.

About the Author

Anthony DiPietro is a gay sex poet and arts administrator originally from Providence, Rhode Island. He has lived throughout New England and in California, New York, Oregon, and Tennessee. A graduate of Brown University with honors in creative writing, he also earned a creative writing MFA at Stony Brook University. Now deputy director of Rose Art Museum at Brandeis University, he resides in Worcester, MA. He composed his 2021 chapbook *And Walk Through* (Seven Kitchens Press) on a typewriter during the pandemic lockdowns. *kiss & release* is his debut collection. His writing and readings are featured on his website, www.AnthonyWriter.com.

About the Press

Unsolicited Press is based out of Portland, Oregon and focuses on the works of the unsung and underrepresented. As a womxn-owned, all-volunteer small publisher that doesn't worry about profits as much as championing exceptional literature, we have the privilege of partnering with authors skirting the fringes of the lit world. We've worked with emerging and award-winning authors such as Shann Ray, Amy Shimshon-Santo, Brook Bhagat, Kris Amos, and John W. Bateman.

Learn more at unsolicitedpress.com. Find us on twitter and instagram.